MW01275517

故宫导游手册

A Guide to the Palace Museum

中国世界语出版社·北京

China Esperanto Press, Beijing, China

First edition: 1996

ISBN 7-5052-0278-2/K.42

Published by China Esperanto Press, Beijing
Distributed by China International Book Trading Corporation
35 Chegongzhuang Xilu, Beijing 100044, China
P.O. Box 399, Beijing, China
Printed in the People's Republic of China

目 录 CONTENTS

前　言

　　故宫是中国明(公元 1368～1644 年)、清(公元 1644～1911 年)两朝皇宫,曾有二十四位皇帝在此处理朝政和居住。它旧称"紫禁城",系借喻紫微星垣而来。中国古代天文学家将天上的恒星分为三垣、二十八宿等星座。三垣包括太微垣、紫微垣和天市垣,紫微垣位居中央,成为代表天帝的星座。天帝居所叫紫宫,人间帝王宫殿借用其名。而皇宫是戒备森严的禁地,故明代称之为"紫禁城"。

　　紫禁城以其悠久的历史、宏大的规模和独具特色的建筑艺术享誉世界。

　　紫禁城的建造始于明初。明朝开国皇帝朱元璋(1368～1398 年在位)于 1368 年在应天府(今江苏省南京市)即位称帝,建号大明,改元洪武。洪武三年,朱元璋封皇四子朱棣为燕王,镇守北平。洪武三十一年朱元璋卒于南京,皇长孙朱允炆继位,是为建文帝。新帝为加强中央集权,采取"削藩"政策,此举激怒了实力雄厚的燕王,他以"靖难"为名,发动了历时四年的"靖难之役",攻陷南京,登上了帝位,改年号为"永乐"。

　　永乐元年(1403 年)正月,朱棣将北平升为陪都,改称北京。永乐四年下诏营建北京宫殿,抽调大批官员、工匠、军士、民夫,分头采木烧砖,整治地基。至永乐十八年,紫禁城告成。这一规模宏大的宫殿建筑群坐落在北京城的南北中轴线上,占地 72 万平方米,共有房舍号称 9999 间半(现存8000 余间),约 15 万平方米,是中国迄今保存最完整的帝王宫阙。

为修建这座巨大的"城中之城",明王朝倾全国人力物力。征集能工巧匠 10 万余名,民夫逾百万。所用建筑材料采自全国各地:木料采自湖广、江西、山西等省;汉白玉石出自北京房山县;墁地金砖烧制于苏州;砌墙用砖来自山东临清。真可谓"量中华之物力,给予人间之仙阙",堪称中国古代宫殿建筑之最。

宫殿竣工后,朱棣于永乐十九年迁都北京。当时紫禁城内三大殿叫奉天、华盖、谨身。朱棣御新殿不到百日,三大殿即被焚毁。他惧怕违背"天意",不敢再建,权以奉天门为听政之所,此后即成为明清两代皇帝相袭的"御门听政"制度。

明代三大殿屡毁屡建。嘉靖四十年(1561 年)重建后,更名为皇极、中极、建极。

满清入关,沿用明朝宫殿。顺治帝(1644～1661 年在位)在位时曾进行较大改建,如按照满族风俗将坤宁宫复修,并将三大殿改名为太和、中和、保和,乾隆帝时多次复修扩建,为其养老的"外东路"(宁寿全宫)即于此时建成。至此,紫禁城方形成今日所见之格局。

紫禁城建筑布局分外朝、内廷两部分。外朝以太和、中和、保和三大殿为主体,左右衔连文华、武英两殿。三大殿以北为内廷,内廷又分中、东、西三路。中为乾清宫、交泰殿、坤宁宫,其后是御花园;中路两侧为东、西六宫。东六宫向北为乾东五所,向南为奉先殿、斋宫、南三所;西六宫往北为乾西五所,往南为养心殿。内廷外围东有宁寿全宫,西有慈宁、寿安诸宫。这种布局,充分体现了古礼所谓"前朝后寝"格局,前朝为"大内正衙",后寝即所谓"三宫六院"。

如此恢宏浩繁的建筑群,所以未给人纷杂之感,主要是在建筑手法上突出了一条极为明显的中轴线。它南起永定门,北至钟鼓楼,全长8公里。皇家禁苑部分约占1/3。整座紫禁城以中轴线为中心展开,天安门为其序幕,外朝三大殿形成高潮,景山是其终曲。整个建筑群体主从分明,跌宕起伏,前后呼应,左右对称,由此形成紫禁城乃至整个北京城的雄伟气魄和井然秩序。

中轴线两边,还伸出了几条次轴线,左有文华——东六宫轴线,右有武英——西六宫轴线,两边又分列宁寿全宫、慈宁诸宫。渐次连接的五条轴线宛如五根金线,将紫禁城纷繁复杂的诸多庭院贯连成五串珍珠,撒在北京城中心,璀璨夺目。

紫禁城作为中国古代建筑的代表作,在艺术处理上有鲜明特点。主要表现在建筑大师们善于将建筑物的各种构件进行艺术加工,从而使构件本身既有实用功能,又有美化建筑物的装饰作用,这突出表现在屋顶上。中国古建筑的屋顶,由于木结构的缘故,形体显得庞大浑厚,为造好大屋顶,聪明的工匠们巧妙地利用木质建筑材料的特点,将整个屋顶做成曲面形,从屋檐到屋的四角都微微翘起,观之如巨鹏展翅,大雁凌云。在长期实践中,中国匠人又创造了庑殿、歇山、攒尖等屋顶形式,以及各种形式交叉组合的复杂形态,如紫禁城角楼,就是这种复杂形态的典型代表。特别值得一提的是,紫禁城殿亭楼阁的屋脊和飞檐上的压脊构件被加工成形态各异的神兽和仙人，它们各自不仅有特定的寓意，而且数量的多寡是建筑物等级的标志。这些外表看似装饰性的构件，还具有必不可少的实用功能。正是由于建筑师们在建造屋顶时从整体到局部都作了艺术加工，突出了民族特色，从而使屋顶成为中国古建筑的主要特征之一，并为世界建筑业在建造同类建筑物时提供了摹仿的范式。

中国古建筑的另一特征，表现为建筑工匠们不但敢于而且善于巧妙设色，他们利用颜色的强烈反差使建筑物主体突出、层次分明。紫禁城宫殿，远望如金波荡漾的浩瀚之海。它以黄绿色为主调，顶盖为黄色琉璃瓦，下饰青绿为主调的彩画，殿身为红墙、红柱、红门窗，底为汉白玉石台基，殿内地面多为绛色。如此大胆地将黄与兰、红与绿、白与黑放在一起，产生了强烈的色彩对比效果，使建筑物的主调鲜明突出，辅调策应生辉，给人以惊心动魄之感。

紫禁城的室内装饰和陈设也别具特色。人们巧妙地利用房屋内部结构、装饰与室内家具、珍宝、字画等物融为一体，用结构与装饰的精美反衬陈设的珍奇与华贵，反之亦然，二者互为表里，相得益彰。在客观上给人的感觉是，无论走进一所殿堂或迈入一方居室，仿佛都是在艺术陈列室中徜徉。如清康乾时代(十七世纪中叶到十八世纪上半叶)的木制家具，以其用料讲究、制作精良、雕刻华美著称于世，成为中国木制家具一绝。精美的家具与室内古色古香的屏风、隔断、博古架相配，即使斗室也不会给人以局促之感，反而使人觉得室内空间宽敞、纵深有序。至于紫禁城的主要殿堂，由于天花板均为大面积的沥粉贴金彩画,天花板正中又有雕刻精妙的金龙藻井,再加上阔门、敞窗、金砖殿面互相辉映,尤显得开阔明亮,恢宏庄严。

尽善尽美的紫禁城里,是否象人们想象的那样天天上演着喜剧呢?并不尽然。明朝末代皇帝崇祯刺伤其女时的一句话:"为何生在帝王家?"道出了几多伤悲、几多无奈?

崇祯十七年三月十八日(1644年2月24日),李自成农民起义军长驱直入北京城,崇祯皇帝走投无路,在乾清宫写下绝命诏书,命周皇后于坤宁宫自尽。接着手提宝剑直奔女儿长平公主的寝宫。十六岁的公主见父皇驾到,忙起身相迎。没等公主站起来,崇祯帝悲伤地说:孩子,你为什么偏偏生在帝王家啊?说完,左手掩面,右手挥剑刺向公主,随后,崇祯帝又砍杀了昭仁公主、袁贵妃及其他妃嫔多人,最后带着满身血迹回到了乾清宫。

绝望之余,仍想求生。崇祯帝换上太监的衣裤靴袜,夹杂在内监数十人中,骑马出了东华门,到守城将军朱纯臣家,朱家未让进府,只好又奔向安定门,安定门关闭日久,铁锁生锈,难于打开。只好返回宫中,鸣钟集合百官,企图作最后的抵抗,竟无一人到来。崇祯皇帝走投无路,于是到万岁山(即今景山)的寿皇亭自缢而死。死时"披发跣左足,右朱履,衣前书曰:'朕自登基十年,逆贼直逼京师,虽朕薄德匪躬,上干天怒,然皆诸臣之误朕也,朕无面目见祖宗于地下,去朕冠冕,以发覆面,任贼分裂朕尸,勿伤百姓一人'"其惨状若此!

紫禁城中还有一位遭受囚禁的皇帝,他就是一生郁郁不得志的光绪皇帝(1874～1908 年在位)。光绪帝名载湉,是醇亲王奕譞和慈禧太后(1835－1908 年)胞妹的儿子,因为同治帝(1861～1874 年在位)晏驾后无子嗣继承大统,而慈禧太后欲立一幼君以便继续把持朝政,故得以入继皇位。他的继位,意味着灾难的开始。载湉入宫时才四岁,没有父母关爱,没有兄姊扶持,在孤独中成长。不仅要遵守各项宫廷礼节,而且经常受到慈禧太后的训斥,从小心情抑郁、精神不快。好不容易捱到了光绪十五年(1889 年)大婚后亲政,慈禧太后迫于祖制,只好退居颐和园"颐养天年"。但是,慈禧太后掌权已逾二十年,权欲熏心,岂肯甘心赋闲。她一方面限制皇帝的权力,重要军国大事均须秉承懿旨办理;一方面又派亲信暗中监视光绪帝的举动,竭力要使他仍成为傀儡。但年轻的皇帝不愿受制于母后,他看到内忧外患的朝局,忧心如焚,力图在政治上有所作为,以挽救岌岌可危的政权。光绪二十四年,开始了"百日维新"。但是,在慈禧太后的干预下,维新变法运动失败了,光绪帝被囚于瀛台。慈禧太后再次训政,多方凌辱折磨光绪帝。起初有谋害之意,而后又想废立。光绪帝亦知其险恶用心,日夕惊忧而又无可奈何,只能提心吊胆,任人宰割。忧能毙人,勉强挣扎了十年,年仅三十八岁的光绪皇帝于慈禧太后去世前一天驾崩了。

　　光绪帝宠爱的珍妃,是清代后妃中死得最惨的。珍妃姓他他拉氏,礼部左侍郎长叙之女,光绪十四年与其姐(即瑾妃)同时被选入宫,次年册封为珍嫔,光绪二十年晋封为珍妃。珍妃美丽贤淑,喜诗善画,深得光绪帝恩宠,引起了慈禧太后的侄女——隆裕皇后的嫉恨。又由于珍妃支持皇帝的政治主张，引起太后盛怒，受到责打，被降为贵人。戊戌变法失败后，珍妃先后被慈禧太后囚禁于建福宫、乾东五所以及颐和园的西一所。后因慈禧太后移居乐寿堂，又将其囚于景祺阁北小院的冷宫里。

据一位老太监回忆说：珍妃关的屋里蛛网满屋，鼠蝎出没，与世隔绝。两三天才由太监隔着门缝送进点食物。珍妃如此苦度了两年，1900年八国联军攻入北京，慈禧太后外逃前命人将她从囚所提出，令其自尽。珍妃不从，太后遂令太监将其推入囚所旁一井中，珍妃抱冤而亡。紫禁城也为之落泪。

1911年辛亥革命后，宣统帝溥仪逊位，退居内廷。外朝部分即三大殿及文华、武英等殿宇归民国政府所有。其时已当上中华民国大总统的袁世凯(1859～1916年)妄图复辟帝制，他选择了紫禁城做舞台，于1915年在这里演了一出袁大"皇帝"的闹剧。

首先，他下令将前朝所有殿宇、门楼匾额上的铜镀金满汉合璧的满文去掉，利用原有的汉文移到匾额中间位置，所以我们今天看故宫，前三殿匾额上均无满文。其次，引经据典修改三大殿殿名，拟将太和、中和、保和三大殿改名为承远、体元、建极，取"承天建极、传之万世"之意。另外，加紧修缮三大殿，改造其内部陈设，以适应新"皇帝"登极需要。据说袁世凯怕太和殿藻井中的轩辕镜掉下伤己，令将地平床向后移，又换掉原来的宝座及宝座两旁的香几、香筒、角端等陈设，换上一把新的雕花嵌大理石宝座，其前置一又高又大的三足鼎式炉、两侧各摆金佛像数尊及佛塔等物，俨如一座佛堂。

登极大典，自然少不了卤簿仪仗，而要做一套全新的已来不及，只好硬着头皮向逊帝借用全套中和韶乐和卤簿仪仗。大典时，新的朝廷命官前来朝贺，许多礼仪和新官员所站方位标志来不及重新制定，于是强行从溥仪处索来品级山，但在使用上却遇到了麻烦。品级山为青铜铸造，由正一品、从一品到正九品、从九品共四套七十二个，每个正面均合铸满汉文某品字样，要将满文去掉，可不象去掉匾额上的满文那么容易，只能将满汉文全部凿掉，另找一块铜板铸好新文字重新镶上。袁世凯别出心裁改正一品为"特任第一班"，但尚未铸"特任第二班"，就连同他的皇帝梦一起夭折了。

紫禁城以其完美的古代建筑艺术、鲜为人知的宫廷秘闻吸引中外游客。这里还藏有大量历史文物和艺术品，其中有许多是稀世绝宝。1925年，紫禁城改名为故宫博物院。新中国成立后，中国政府每年拨巨款对它进行保护和维修。现在的故宫，已成为中国最负盛名的旅游热点。

Foreword

The former Imperial Palace, also known as the Forbidden City, was the residence to 24 emperors of the Ming and Qing dynasties from 1420 to 1911. Now it is open as the Palace Museum.

Zhu Yuanzhang founded the Ming Dynasty in 1368 and set his capital in Nanjing. He made his fourth son Zhu Di the Prince of Yan and commander of Beijing garrison. Zhu Yuanzhang died in 1398. His grandson Zhu Yunwen succeeded him. The new emperor wanted to reduce the power of local garrison commanders, most of whom were royal family members. Zhu Di, enraged, staged a revolt and usurped the throne from his nephew. Beijing became his second capital.

In 1406 Emepror Yong Le (Zhu Di) ordered the construction of the palace in Beijing. A hundred thousand artisans and a million workmen were conscripted on the project. Wood were sent from southern provinces, marble cut at Fangshan in Beijing's outskirts, bricks for paving the ground baked in Suzhou, Jiangsu Province, and bricks for the walls made in Linqing, Shandong Province. The new palace was completed in 1420.

Zhu Di formally moved his capital from Nanjing to Beijing in 1422. But in no more than 100 days after he took residence in the new palace, the three main halls in the Outer Court were burnt down. The emperor believed the disaster was caused by divine power and dared not to rebuild the halls. He decided to hold court in the tower of Fengtian Gate.

Later Ming emperors rebuilt the three main halls several times, but they were all destroyed by natural disasters again.

The last overall reconstruction during the Ming Dynasty was carried out in 1561 during the reign of Emperor Jia Jing.

The Manchus took Beijing in 1644 and established the Qing Dynasty. During the reign of Shun Zhi between 1644 and 1661 a large-scale renovation of the Imperial Palace was undertaken. The Palace of Earthly Tranquility was rebuilt according to the customs of the Manchus. The three main halls were renamed Taihe, Zhonghe and Baohe. Emperor Qian Long continued to expand the Imperial Palace and built the Outer Eastern Palaces for himself to stay after he retired from the throne. Since then the Imperial Palace has seen little change in construction and layout.

The construction of the Imperial Palace followed strictly the mythological philosophy and astrology of ancient China. The direction, shape and ornamentation of each group of buildings or individual buildings all bear certain significance.

The Imperial Palace is composed of the Outer Court and Inner Court. In the Outer Court along a single axis are the three main halls: the Hall of Supreme Harmony (Taihedian), the Hall of Central Harmony (Zhonghedian), and the Hall of Preserving Harmony (Baohedian). On either side of them are two minor halls: the Hall of Literary Glory (Wenhuadian), and the Hall of the Martial Spirit (Wuyingdian).

The buildings in the Inner Court are arranged along three routes. On the central line are the three main halls: the Palace of Heavenly Purity (Qianqinggong), the Hall of Union (Jiaotaidian), and the Palace of Earthly Tranquility (Kunninggong). At the northern end of this line is the Imperial Garden. Parallel to the central line are the Six Western Palaces and the Six Eastern Palaces. To the south of the Six Eastern Palaces are the Hall of Worshipping Ancestors (Fengxiandian), the Palace of Abstinency (Zhaigong) and Nansansu; to the south of the Six Western Palaces is the Hall of Mental Cultivation (Yangxindian). On the eastern side of the three main halls is the Palace of Tranquil Longevity (Ningshougong); on the western side are the Palace of Motherly Tranquility (Cininggong), and the Palace of Longevity and Peace (Shou'angong).

The entire palace area, rectangular in shape and 720,000 square meters in size, takes up one-third of the 8-kilometer-long central axis of the old Beijing city from the city gate of Yongdingmen on the south to the Drum and Bell Towers on the north. This harmonious assemblage of buildings displays the best characteristics of Chinese architecture—majestic style, flawless construction, fine coordination of the whole and the parts.

Most of ancient buildings in China have large wooden roofs with upturned eaves. They fall in several types such as Wudian hipped roof, gabled roof and capered roof. A representative masterpiece is the Corner Tower at each of the four corners of the Imperial Palace. The zoomorphic ornaments (*liwen*) on the roof ridges in the palace deserve particular mention. They are in the shapes of divine animals and immortals. Their number on the roof ridge is decided by the importance of the building—the more important a building the larger is the number. Another feature of the Imperial Palace is the bold application of colors. The dominant colors are yellow and dark green: yellow glazed roof tiles and large stretches of dark green in the ornamental painting. The walls, pillars and windows are painted vermilion. The halls stand on white marble terraces. Such sharp color contrast is against the usual concept that colors should be combined on a graduation basis.

The furniture, treasures and works of painting and calligraphy are arranged to merge with the interior as a whole. One feels entering an art display in every building. The wooden furniture such as treasure shelves, partition screens and tables and chairs made during the reign of Emperor Kang Xi of the Qing Dynasty from the mid-17th to the early 18th century in the Imperial Palace are masterpieces. They are famous for their elaborate carvings and meticulous workmanship. With all these furniture in the room one does not feel crowded. The gilded ceiling and the coffered ceiling in the center, wide doors, large windows and golden paved floor make the main halls in the Imperial Palace seem more spacious than they actually are.

To the common people the emperor and his family must lead the most luxurious life in the Imperial Palace. In fact, the Imperial Palace in Beijing saw many tragedies. On February 24, 1644, the peasant insurgent army led by Li Zicheng entered Beijing. Emperor Chong Zhen ordered his empress to commit suicide and then went to the palace of his 16-year-old daughter who came up to greet him. Before he thrust the sword into the girl's body he said, "Why was you born into the imperial house!?" He went on to kill his another daughter and several of his concubines.

But the emperor did not want to die. He disguised himself as a eunuch and fled on a horse, only to find nowhere to escape. He returned to the palace to summon his officials for a last-ditch struggle. No one came to his call. All hope lost, the emperor hanged himself at the foot of the Coal Hill behind the palace. Before he died he wrote on a piece of cloth torn off his robe: "For ten years I sat on the throne. Bandits forced their way to the city wall of the capital. Although I deserved the punishment of the Heavenly wrath for my inadequate virtue, the court officials should be blamed for my mistakes. I am ashamed to meet my ancestors underground. So I took off my crown and covered my face with my hair. The bandits may cut my body to pieces. But I ask you not to hurt the common people."

Emperor Guang Xu was on the throne between 1874 and 1908. He was the son of a prince. Emperor Tong Zhi (reigned between 1861 and 1874) died without a son. Empress Dowager Ci Xi put Guang Xu (4 years old then) on the throne. The child was constantly chided and scolded by the powerful Ci Xi. In 1889 he was formally allowed to attend to state affairs. But Ci Xi continued to rule the country and made Guang Xu a puppet. In an attempt to take over the real power and save the collapsing country, the young emperor launched a political reform, only to be defeated by the die-hard bureaucrats led by Empress Dowager Ci Xi. The emperor was put under house arrest for ten years before he died at the age of 38.

Zhenfei, a favorite concubine of Emperor Guang Xu, beautiful and well learned, supported the emperor's reform.

She was thus disliked by both the empress and Empress Dowager Ci Xi. She was first put in confinement. In 1900 the Allied Forces of Eight Foreign Powers invaded Beijing. Before the royal family fled Empress Dowager Ci Xi ordered Zhenfei to take her own life. Zhenfei refused. Ci Xi then ordered a eunuch to push Zhenfei into a well. The young woman was drowned.

The 1911 Revolution overthrew the Qing Dynasty. Emperor Xuan Tong was allowed to stay in the Inner Court. Part of the Outer Court became offices of the new Republic government. But Yuan Shikai (1859-1916), the Republic president, enthroned himself as Emperor Hong Xian in 1915. He had the Hall of Supreme Harmony refurbished for the occasion, changing all the bilingual (Han and Manchu) inscriptions into the Han language. He also removed the horizontal board over the throne and the couplet on the pillars. For fear that the glass balls above the throne might drop and injure him, he had the dais and the throne moved backwards to where it is now. In order to make his enthronement "authentic" he borrowed from the abdicated emperor of the Qing Dynasty whole sets of musicians and ceremony ministers and companions. His monarchy lasted only 80 days, ending with his death.

The former Imperial Palace keeps a great quantity of historic relics and artistic objects. In 1925 it was turned into a museum. Since the founding of the People's Republic in 1949 the central government has repaired and renovated it on several occasions. It allots large sums every year for its maintenance. Now it is a hot tourist attraction in China.

外 朝

紫禁城以乾清门前横街为界分为外朝、内廷两大部分。外朝的中心建筑是太和、中和、保和三大殿，是皇帝举行各种重大典礼的地方。

朝会是朝廷最为隆重的典礼活动。清朝沿袭明制，每逢皇帝即位、大婚、册立皇后以及元旦、冬至、万寿节（皇帝的生日）等日子，皇帝都要到太和殿接受文武百官和外国使臣的祝贺。

举行朝贺仪式时，从太和殿露台起陈列仪仗旗帜，连续不断地南出午门一直排列到天安门外。太和殿广场设有仪马百匹，卤簿（仪仗）人员一千零六十三人；太和门外陈设步辇，卤簿人员六十六人；午门外陈设玉、金、象、木、革五辂和驮宝瓶的驯象，卤簿人员四百一十七人；天安门外卤簿人员三十一人，共有卤簿人员一千五百七十七人。如此规模的卤簿，在世界各国皇家仪仗中，当位列第一。

銮仪卫陈列卤簿的同时，乐部将由编钟、编磬、琴、瑟、箫、笙等乐器组成的中和韶乐设在太和殿东西檐下，把由云锣、方响、管子、杖鼓等乐器组成的丹陛大乐设在太和门内东西檐下。礼部将王公百官的贺表陈列在太和殿内东侧案上，把各省官员的贺表放在午门外龙亭内。

文武百官则必须于日出前，在午门外排班站好等候。到时辰再由礼部官员导引，文左武右从左右掖门进入太和殿广场东西两侧，按正、从九品分十八班站好，等候皇帝御殿。

届时，皇帝着明黄色朝服，乘舆出宫，午门鸣钟鼓，至保和殿降舆。先到中和殿升座，接受侍班、执事、导从等典礼执事人员叩拜。然后进入太和殿，在中和韶乐声中升宝座。在丹陛大乐伴奏下，文武百官跪下，山呼万岁。乐止，宣表官宣读贺表毕，再奏丹陛大乐，文武百官行三跪九叩礼。然后皇帝降座，奏中和韶乐，退朝还宫。

　　清朝末代皇帝溥仪于光绪三十四年十一月初九日（1908年12月2日）在太和殿即位时，年仅三岁，由他的父亲摄政王载沣抱扶在宝座上，载沣单膝侧身跪在宝座下。传说大典进行时，热闹庄严的场面吓得小皇帝哭闹不止，叫喊："我要回家！"载沣随口劝说："不要哭，一会儿就完了。"事后，大臣们狐疑这话不吉利。后来，溥仪果然只作了三年皇帝便逊位了。

　　窃取了辛亥革命胜利果实的袁世凯，为了筹办1916年元旦的登基大典，将太和殿改名为"承远殿"。又因自己腿短，攀坐原来的宝座不方便，遂换成一把中西结合、椅背极高的大椅。袁世凯称帝失败后，椅子弃之不用，逐渐损坏。1959年在故宫库房中发现了已破损不堪的宝座，经修整后，恢复了历史的原貌。

The Outer Court

The Imperial Palace grounds are divided into the Outer Court and the Inner Court by the Gate of Heavenly Purity. The main structures of the Outer Court are the Hall of Supreme Harmony (Taihedian), the Hall of Central Harmony (Zhonghedian) and the Hall of Preserving Harmony (Baohedian). They were where the emperor held official audiences, award ceremonies, weddings, birth celebrations and official banquets. The emperor received greetings from attending officials and foreign envoys in the Hall of Supreme Harmony.

Other grand ceremonies were also held in the Outer Court such as on New Year's Day, Winter Solstice, Longevity Festival, proclamation of imperial edicts, the enthronement of the empress, receiving successful candidates of the imperial examination, and appointment of commander-in-chief of expedition troops during a war. On an important occasion, the central pathway from the Gate of Heavenly Peace (Tian'anmen), through the Meridian Gate (Wumen) to the marble terrace of the Hall of Supreme Harmony was lined with flags, weapons, shields, parasols, fans and gold and silver decorations. In the spacious courtyard of the Hall of Supreme Harmony 100 horses and a 1,063-men guard of honor stood in neat formation; 66 attendants with the emperor's sedan chair stood outside the Gate of Supreme Harmony; outside the Meridian Gate there were five ceremonial chariots and 417 attendants; outside the Gate of Heavenly Peace there were 31 guards. Gold bells, jade qing (a kind of percussion instrument), flute, zither, drum and many other kinds of musical instruments formed two large orchestras which were placed outside the Hall of

Supreme Harmony. The Minister of Rites placed the letters of congratulation from court officials and nobles on a desk in the Eastern Chamber of the Hall of Supreme Harmony and the letters of congratulation from provincial officials in the Dragon Pavilion outside the Meridian Gate.

All the officials attending a grand ceremony had to arrive at the Meridian Gate before dawn, then were led by officials of the Board of Rites into the courtyard of the Hall of Supreme Harmony. They took their places designated to them by bronze "position markers" according to each's official rank.

When time arrived the bell and drum at the Meridian Gate were struck. The emperor in yellow ceremonial dress was carried on a sedan chair to the Hall of Preserving Harmony. From there he walked to the Hall of Middle Harmony to receive the greetings of attendants and officials of the Board of Rites. After that he went to the Hall of Supreme Harmony to ascend the throne amidst music. All people present would kneel and shout "Longevity". The Master of Ceremony read the paper of tribute. Music struck again. Officials kowtowed to the emperor. The emperor stepped down from the throne and retired to the rear part of the Imperial Palace.

When the last emperor of the Qing Dynasty Aisin Gioro Pu Yi was enthroned in the Hall of Supreme Harmony on December 2, 1908, he was only a child of three. While the ceremony was going on the boy emperor became fidgeting and kept crying. His father, Prince Regent Zaifeng, was kneeling below the throne. As the boy emperor kept crying, "I don't like it here. I want to go home." he tried to soothe him by saying,

"Don't cry. It'll be over soon." After the ceremony officials in their surreptitious gossip took these words as an evil omen. These words proved to be prophetic, as within three years, the Qing Dynasty was finished.

Not long after the Revolution of 1911 which overthrew the Qing Dynasty, Yuan Shikai usurped state power and ehthroned himself as Emperor Hong Xian on December 12, 1915. He changed the name of the Hall of Supreme Harmony to Chengyuan (To Carry Far). For fear that the glass balls hanging from the ceiling might drop and injure him, he had the dais and the throne moved backwards to where it is now. He also replaced the throne with one specially made to suit his short legs. The throne on display today is the original one of the Ming Dynasty. It was discovered in the imperial stock in 1959.

故宫远眺

角楼 故宫城墙四隅各设角楼一座，它们均为六个歇山顶组合而成的奇特整体。每楼三层屋檐设计有二十八个翼角，七十二条屋脊，造型精巧玲珑，堪称中国古建一绝。

Corner Tower At each of the four corners of the palace stands a unique tower, each with six hipped and gabled roofs. The three-tiered eaves sloping into 28 upturning curves, together with 10 gables and 72 ridges, add much grace to the structure.

29

午门 　为紫禁城正门，它高35.6米，座落于京城南北中轴线上，居中向阳，位当子午，故名午门。城台上建崇楼五座，俗称"五凤楼"。门分五洞，中门供皇帝出入，叫"御路"；王公大臣走左右门；掖门平时不开，唯逢太和殿大典，文武百官分别从左右掖门入；殿试时，考生按单双号分进左右掖门。

eridian Gate (Wumen) It is he largest gate of the palace nd stands on the central axis f Beijing City. Surmounted y five pavilions, this mas- ive gate is also known as the Five-Phoenix Tower ". The ate has five openings. The central one was used exclu- sively by the emperor. Court officials passed through the two gates near the central one. The two sidegates were opened only to let in success- ful candidates of imperial ex- aminations.

31

内金水河 午门内即太和门广场。内金水河象广场腰间一条皎净无暇的缎带悄悄飘流。它源于北京西郊的泉水之乡——玉泉山，从故宫西北角地沟流入宫中，河道弯弯曲曲，水碧似玉，得名玉带河。

Inner Golden Water River Fed by spring water from Yuquan Hill on the western outskirts of Beijing, the canal runs from northwestern corner and through the palace. It is also called "Jade Belt River" for its clear water of emerald color.

太和门 是外朝三大殿的正门,为宫中等级最高的门。明、清两朝均有"御门听政"之制,即文武官员早朝,皇帝接受臣下朝拜和处理政事的制度。清康熙帝(1661～1722年在位)以前的皇帝均在此门听政。

Gate of Supreme Harmony (Tai-hemen) This main entrance to the Outer Court is the tallest of all gates in the palace. Before the reign of Emperor Kang Xi (1661-1722) it served the emperor as a reception hall for ministers.

俯瞰外朝三大殿 太和、中和、保和三大殿是故宫的核心建筑,它们座落在三层重叠的"工"字形丹陛上,威严壮丽,气势非凡。

Bird's-eye view of the three main halls The imposing imperial halls stand on a three-tiered marble terrace. They are the main part of the Imperial Palace.

铜狮　太和门前左右两侧各设铜狮一尊，左雄右雌，威武凶悍。雄狮右足踏绣球，象征权力和一统天下；雌狮左足抚幼狮，象征子嗣昌盛。故宫共有六对铜狮，唯太和门前这对最大。

Bronze Lions Two bronze lions are placed at either side of the Gate of Supreme Harmony. The one on the west side is female with a baby lion under its left paw, symbolizing fertility of the royal family; the one on the east is male with an embroidered ball under its right paw, symbolizing the imperial power.

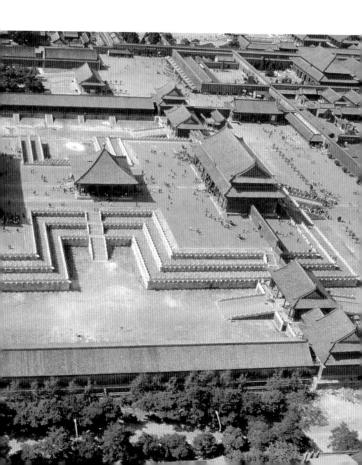

丹陛 为汉白玉石雕砌而成，共三层，通高8.13米。每层丹陛均横卧地袱，绕以汉白玉石栏杆，上立望柱1458根，柱头精雕云龙云凤图案。地袱下设排水沟，沟口雕制蚣蝮1142个，每至雨天，千龙喷水，蔚为壮观。

Danbi（Imperial Terrace） The three main halls of the palace stand on a vast three-tiered marble terrace which is 8.13 meters high and edged with 1,458 white marble balusters carved with patterns of dragons and phoenixes. At the base of these balustrades are 1,142 gargoyles in the shape of dragon head which make a spectacle during a downpour.

太和殿广场 广场占地三万多平方米,正中为巨石铺成的"御路",其左右为磨砖对缝的海墁砖地。御道两旁设置铜制品级山,每逢大典,文东武西,诸大臣按官阶跪于品阶山旁;各国使臣亦按指定位置跪拜。

Square of the Hall of Supreme Harmony The open ground in front of the Hall of Supreme Harmony covers more than 30,000 square meters. The central "Imperial Road" is paved with large stone slabs and the rest with bricks. On major occasions, bronze markers were placed along the sides of the "Imperial Road" and court officials knelt in the order of ranks. Foreign envoys knelt at their designated spot.

太和殿 为故宫第一大殿,俗称金銮殿,始建于明永乐四年(1406 年),现存建筑系康熙三十四年(1695 年)所修。它面阔十一间,进深五间,通高 35.5 米,总面积达 2300 平方米,是中国现存最大的木结构建筑。明、清两代皇帝即位、大婚、册立皇后以及元旦赐宴、命将出征和金殿传胪等大典均在此举行。

Hall of Supreme Harmony (Tai-hedian) Commonly known as the Hall of Gold Throne, the magnificent structure was built in 1406 and renovated in 1695. It is 35.5 meters high and has a floor space of 2,300 square meters with 182 beams and 84 pillars. It is the largest wood structure extant in China. During the Ming and Qing dyansties grand ceremonies such as the enthronement of the emperor, New Year's Day, proclamation of imperial edicts, receiving successful candidates of imperial examination, appointment of commander-in-chief of expedition troops were held here.

太和殿内景 殿内陈设保持着当年帝、后临朝原状。正中为七级高台的地平床,上设屏风、宝座、御案,两侧有对称的宝象、角端、仙鹤、香炉等珐琅制品。殿内金碧辉煌,庄严华贵。

Inside the Hall of Supreme Harmony The interior of the Gold Throne Hall is preserved as in ancient times. On the raised platform is the gilded imperial throne placed on a dais two meters high. Behind the throne is a carved screen. On either side of the throne are a crane-shaped candle-stick, an elephant-shaped incense burner and a column-shaped incense burner with a pagoda on top which are all cloisonne wares.

宝座 是皇权的象征。太和殿内宝座为故宫诸多宝座之魁。其上半部为圈椅靠背，背上金龙缠绕，下部为金漆蟠龙须弥座。座后设有七扇雕龙髹金屏风。

Throne The painted golden throne with a splendid screen behind it stands on a two-meter high dais in the center of the Hall of Supreme Harmony. Its back and the lower part are covered with coiled dragons. This is the most magnificent of all the thrones in the palace.

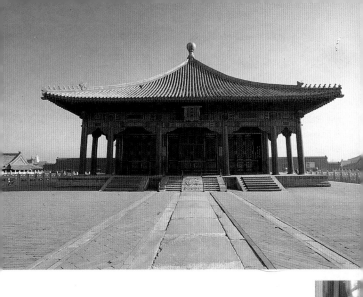

肩舆 中和殿内陈列肩舆两
座,图为其一。肩舆俗称轿子,
是清代皇帝在宫内使用的交通
工具,有礼舆、步舆、轻步舆、便
舆四种,平时皇帝在宫廷园囿
出入均乘便舆。

Sedan Chair The emperor was
carried on a sedan chair to
travel inside the Imperial
Palace. His sedan chairs came
into four types according to
the occasion they were used:
ceremonial chair, walking
chair, light walking chair
and casual chair. The casual
chair was mostly used.

中和殿　位于太和殿后,为深广各五间的方形殿,其顶为单檐四角攒尖鎏金宝顶,象征天圆地方。当时,皇帝去太和殿举行大典前在此小憩,接受内阁、礼部及侍卫执事人员的朝拜。此外,祭坛庙前阅视祭文,亲耕前验看种子和农具,审阅皇室玉牒等活动也在此举行。

Hall of Middle Harmony (Zhonghedian) The square hall with a pyramidic roof stands behind the Hall of Supreme Harmony. The emperor would take a rest and receive greetings from attendants and officials of the Board of Rites before he went to the Hall of Supreme Harmony. He also practiced rites for worshipping ceremonies and examined crop seeds and farm tools in this hall before he personally did some field work.

保和殿　是外朝最后的大殿
面阔九间,进深五间,寓意"
五之尊"。明朝册立皇后、
子,大臣称贺上表,皇帝在此
上衮冕再到太和殿受贺,并
此殿大宴群臣。清朝皇帝在
筵宴王公、额附;乾隆帝(17
～1795 年在位)以后在此举
殿试,选拔贤才。

all of Preserving Harmony Baohedian) The last of the three main halls in the Outer Court is nine bays wide and five bays deep. In the Ming Dynasty, before going to the ceremony of granting title on the empress or the crown prince, the emperor would change into full ceremonial dress in this hall. In the Qing Dynasty, the emperor gave banquet in honor of Uygur and Mongol nobles. From 1789 onward the final session of the Civil Service Examinations was held in this hall with the supervision of the emperor.

云龙雕石　位于保和殿后，为故宫最大的石雕。它由一整块艾叶青石雕成，长 16.57 米，宽 3.07 米，重约 250 吨。下端雕有海水江崖，中间九条蟠龙行踞于流云之中，神态自然，矫健生动。此雕石选材之巨，构图设计之妙，雕凿之精，鲜有出其右者。

Dragon-Cloud Jade Carving It is placed behind the Hall of Preserving Harmony. The largest carving in the Palace Museum was first made during the Ming Dynasty. It was re-carved during the Qing Dynasty. It is 16.75 meters long and 3.07 meters wide. On it are exquisite designs of mountain cliffs, sea waves, clouds and nine dragons.

后 三 宫

　　三大殿以北为内廷,内廷又分中、东、西三路。中为乾清宫、交泰殿、坤宁宫,俗称后三宫,是帝后生活的重心。"乾"即"天",代表皇帝,"坤"即"地",代表皇后;"乾清"、"坤宁"寓意皇帝政治清明,皇后守礼辅佐,则可统治长久。"交泰"象征天地交泰、帝后和睦。

　　而大婚则是乾得坤,达到乾清坤宁的途径。

　　封建社会,皇帝结婚立后,称为大婚。届时要举行盛大而繁缛的礼仪活动。大婚前,先要由皇太后和近支王妃、皇戚通过数年的议婚选定皇后,接着要行纳彩礼、大征礼、奉迎礼、合卺礼、庆贺礼、赐宴礼等一大套礼仪。

　　纳彩,就是皇帝向皇后娘家赠送具有定婚意义的礼物,主要有马匹、甲胄、丝绸、布帛、金茶筒、银盆等。择吉日,由正、副使率领庞大的送礼队伍送往皇后家。

　　接着举行大征礼,也就是皇帝在迎娶皇后入宫前,再一次向皇后家赠送礼品。除固定数目的马匹外,还要赠黄金二百两,白银万两,缎千疋和金、银茶具等。

　　最隆重的仪式当数册封、奉迎礼。头一天,皇帝须遣官祭告天地、太庙。奉迎之日,京城内外家家张灯结彩,以示庆贺。紫禁城内更是一片喜庆景象:红毡铺路,殿堂宫门粉刷一新,到处悬挂双喜红绸,高悬双喜宫灯。当天早晨太和殿内设节案、册案和宝案,殿外陈设皇帝法驾卤簿,太和殿檐下设中和韶乐,太和门内檐下陈丹陛大乐。慈宁宫外陈皇太后仪驾,太和门外至午门陈皇后仪驾。吉时一到,礼部堂官恭导皇帝穿礼服出宫,先赴慈宁宫向太后行礼,再在太和殿升座,遣使持节去皇后府邸行册立皇后之礼,并奉迎皇后入宫。

长长的奉迎仪仗,导引着皇后凤舆(即喜轿)绕行大半个京城,最后由大清门、天安门、端门到午门。仪驾停在天安门外。皇后凤舆在九凤曲柄盖前导下进午门、经太和门、中左门、后左门到乾清门,在乾清宫前降舆。由内监执提炉前导,皇后步行入乾清宫到后隔扇,改乘八人孔雀顶轿到钟粹宫,等候入坤宁宫洞房。

坤宁宫东暖阁即是大婚洞房。迎门竖有一座大红底金字"囍"字木影壁,取帝后合卺"开门见喜"之意。暖阁里间靠北墙是龙凤喜床,南边窗前一铺大炕则是举行合卺礼的地方。举行合卺礼时,皇后先由儿女双全的福晋命妇四人扶持,从钟粹宫到坤宁宫。随后,皇帝穿吉服入洞房。皇帝居左,皇后居右,对面而坐。由福晋命妇恭侍帝、后进合卺宴。帝后对饮交杯酒时,另有结发侍卫夫妇在宫外唱"交祝歌"。宴毕礼成,众人散去,帝后始得安歇。

第二天(或过几天),帝、后分别去慈宁宫拜见皇太后。皇帝还要在太和殿设大朝庆贺礼。届时,文武百官、外国使臣进表祝贺,皇帝颁诏,布告天下,然后,皇帝在太和殿、皇太后在慈宁宫分别赐宴皇后父、母及诸臣命妇,并赏礼物,大婚礼成。

最后,为庆祝皇帝大婚,宫中要连续演戏三天。皇帝、皇后、妃嫔以及太后、王公大臣都要前往观戏,京师名角都须进宫献艺。

在清朝入关后的十个皇帝中,末代皇帝溥仪逊位时尚不满六岁,不能成婚立后。雍正、乾隆、嘉庆、道光、咸丰五个皇帝,都是在婚后继位的,只须将原嫡福晋册立为皇后,不需再行大婚礼。通过行大婚礼册立皇后的,只有幼年继位的顺治、康熙、同治、光绪四个皇帝。

The Inner Court

Behind the three great halls of the Outer Court is a long open ground running from east to west, which serves as a demarcation line between the Outer Court and the Inner Court. The emperor lived in the Inner Court with his empress and scores of concubines, served by thousands of palace maids and eunuchs. The buildings in the Inner Court, like those in the Outer Court, are arranged along three lines.

The emperor's wedding was an important event. An extremely magnificent wedding ceremony would be held in the Inner Court. First, the empress dowager would confer with royal family members and ministers on the choice of the future empress. Then a series of complicated and costly ceremonies were performed. The betrothal gifts were sent to the bride's house, which included horses, suits of armour, bolts of silk, gold tea containers and silver tea sets. Before the wedding wedding gifts were sent to the bride's house, which included 200 taels of gold, 10,000 taels of silver, and gold and silver tea containers.

The Ceremony of Crowning and Welcoming the Empress was the most grandiose ceremony during the celebration of the emperor's marriage. On that day huge red lanterns hung everywhere inside the Imperial Palace. Temporary ceremonial gateways adorned with "double happiness" were put up in front of the Gate of Supreme Harmony, the Hall of Supreme Harmony, the Palace of Heavenly Purity and the Palace of Earthly Tranquility. The door-gods and couplets were repainted and the columns of the palace halls were entwined with gold dragons and red phoenixes. The emperor in ceremonial robes first went to the empress dowager's palace to pay homage to her and then came to the Hall of Supreme Harmony to have a look at the appointment of empress. An imperial envoy dispatched by the emperor went to the empress's house, where he was accorded warm welcome by the empress and her mother. Certificate and the seal of the empress were presented to the empress. Soon after this ceremony, the empress was escorted to the Imperial Palace. The imperial envoy on horseback was at the head of the royal procession, followed by the guards of honor and the empress's palanquin. Four ladies rode on horses ahead of the palanquin and seven ladies behind it. The royal mounted police force took charge of the security all along the route. The empress's palanquin passed through the Great Qing Gate, the Gate of Heavenly Peace, the Meridian Gate, the Gate of Supreme Harmony, and finally stopped at the Palace of Heavenly Purity, where she changed to another palanquin with a phoenix design on top and was carried by eight guards to the Palace of Quintessence.

Soon afterwards the empress, accompanied by four bridemaids, came to the Palace of Earthly Tranquility in a sedan chair. In the Eastern Warm Chamber, the emperor and the empress were seated facing each other on the bridal bed. Then the bridemaids served the wedding dinner and the bride and the bridegroom drank the nuptial wine. The gold wine cups were decorated with red and green threads symbolizing everlasting happiness and longevity. In the mean time, a choir composed of married couples sang love songs outside the chamber.

On the second day the emperor and the empress paid a formal visit to the empress dowager. On the 4th day an imposing ceremony was held in the Hall of Supreme Harmony. All the high-ranking officials and foreign envoys were present, extending their greetings to the emperor. Operas were staged in the palace for three days.

Since its conquest of the whole country, the Qing Dynasty had ten emperors in power, of whom five emperors (Yong Zheng, Qian Long, Jia Qing, Dao Guang and Xian Feng) ascended the throne after they were married. Therefore their consorts became the empresses in the wake of the succession. Naturally there were no wedding ceremony in this case. Four emperors (Shun Zhi, Kang Xi, Tong Zhi and Guang Xu) were married after they were enthroned. Pu Yi, the last emperor of the Qing Dynasty, abdicated at the age of six. So he had no imperial wedding ceremony.

乾清门 是内廷正门。门为五楹大殿,三洞朱门设于后檐柱间。由于门厅宽阔宏丽,清代自康熙皇帝起,将太和门的"御门听政"改在此处。

Gate of Heavenly Purity (Qian-qingmen) The Gate of Heavenly Purity, built like a mansion, is the main entrance to the Inner Court. Beginning from Emperor Kang Xi, the Qing emperors sometimes gave audience to government officials at this gate

乾清宫 是内廷正殿,宽九间,深五间,重檐庑殿顶,梁枋饰金龙和玺彩画,为内廷等级最高的宫殿。这里是明朝和清朝顺治、康熙皇帝的寝宫,也是皇帝处理日常政务的地方。皇帝驾崩,停灵柩于殿内。

Palace of Heavenly Purity (Qianqinggong) The double-eaved building rises 24 meters high and is decorated with minute paintings. It is the most important building in the Inner Court. During the Ming Dynasty and the reign of Shun Zhi and Kang Xi of the Qing Dynasty, it served as the living quarters of the emperor, who also attended state affairs here. The dead emperor was also laid in state in this palace.

乾清宫内景 殿内中央方形地平床上设金漆雕龙宝座和屏风,其上悬"正大光明"横匾,这是清代自雍正皇帝(1722～1735年在位)以后,在位皇帝为避免皇子间争夺皇位继承权而秘藏立储遗诏的地方。

Inside the Palace of Heavenl Purity In the center of th main hall there is a squar platform with a throne and a ornate dragon screen, both c which are gold painted ar decorated with delicate carv ings. High up in the middle c the hall there is a plaqu

with an inscription which reads "Be open and above-board". The emperors of the Qing Dynasty after Emperor Yong Zheng would write the name of his successor, put the paper in a box and hide the box behind the plaque. The box was opened when the emperor died, thus avoiding competition among his sons.

交泰殿 位于乾清宫后,规制如中和殿。殿名寓意天地交泰,帝后和睦。皇后逢大典及生日在此受贺。亲蚕前,皇后在此设斋戒牌和斋戒铜人,并阅视篮子、勾子等用具。乾隆帝以后,这里是存放二十五宝的地方。

Hall of Union (Jiaotaidian)
Located between the Palace of Heavenly Purity and the Palace of Earthly Tranquility, the interior of this hall is similar to that of the Hall of Middle Harmony. Its name means "Heaven and earth are united", symbolizing the harmonious relationship between the emperor and the empress. Birthday celebrations of the empress were held in this hall. In spring the empress presided a ceremony to begin the silkworm breeding season.

玺 存放于交泰殿内地平床两边和宝座两侧。玺，即印，本为统称，自秦(公元前221～前206年)以后，专指皇帝之印。交泰殿内存有乾隆年间鉴定的宝玺二十五方。取二十五之数，源于《周易》"天数二十有五"之说，似有祈求上苍保佑"大清得享国号二十有五"之意，然清入关后实传十代而告终。

Imperial Seals Twenty-five imperial seals of the Qing emperors are kept in the Hall of Union. Emperor Qian Long hoped that by keeping 25 seals, the Qing Dynasty could rule the country for at least 25 generations. Nevertheless, his prayers did not work. The Qing Dynasty only lasted to the 10th generation after the Manchus established their capital in Beijing.

坤宁宫 为明、清两朝皇后的寝宫。"坤宁"与"乾清"象征天清地宁统治长久。1644 年农民军领袖李自成率兵攻入北京，崇祯皇帝(1627～1644 年在位)的周皇后自尽于此宫。清代自雍正帝以后，皇帝由乾清宫迁往养心殿居住，皇后也改居东西六宫的某一宫。

Palace of Earthly Tranquility (Kunninggong) It was the residence of the empress during the Ming and Qing times. In 1644 when the peasant uprising leader Li Zicheng seized

Beijing, Empress Zhou of Emperor Chong Zhen (1627-1644)
committed suicide here. After
Yong Zheng, the Qing emperors
moved their residence to the
Hall of Mental Cultivation
and the empresses moved their
residence to one of the Six
Eastern Palaces or one of the
Six Western Palaces.

坤宁宫内景　中国满族礼重祀神,凡祭必于正寝,清顺治十二年(1655年)袭盛京清宁宫旧俗,将坤宁宫中部四间大堂改为萨满教祭神场所。祭礼分日祭、月祭、春秋大祭等,大祭之日帝、后临场。图中宝座为皇帝祭神时吃祭肉的座位。

Inside the Palace of Earthly Tranquility The ruling class of the Qing Dynasty attached great importance to worshipping the God of Rites. In 1655 Emperor Shun Zhi turned four halls of this palace into a shrine for Shaman gods. Sacrificial ceremonies were held here in honor of the Sun, the Moon, in spring and autumn. The emperor and empress came in person. The throne in the picture was for the emperor to sit on when he ate the sacrificial meat.

大婚洞房　坤宁宫按满族风俗改建后，殿东两间暖阁为皇帝大婚洞房，婚后帝、后仅在此住两夜，第三天皇帝回养心殿，皇后则在东西六宫中任择一宫居住。今阁内陈设保留光绪皇帝大婚原状。

Bridal Chamber After the renovation of the Palace of Earthly Tranquility according to Manchu's customs the anteroom to the east of the main hall became the bridal chamber. The emperor and empress would stay in this place for two nights after the wedding. Then the emperor went to live in the Hall of Mental Cultivation and the empress went to stay in one of the Six Eastern Palaces or one of the Six Western Palaces. The bridal chamber has preserved the same decoration as used at the wedding of Emperor Guang Xu.

养心殿和西六宫

后三宫西南为养心殿,清朝,这里是除太和殿以外最重要的地方。自雍正皇帝以后,皇帝在此处理政务和居住。

养心殿是工字形建筑,前殿后殿相连,周围廊庑环抱,比较紧凑,前殿办事,后殿就寝,舒适自如。前殿正间,是皇帝召见大臣、引见官员的地方。凡是官员升迁、补缺、调动或任期到一定年限,由吏部尚书带领,跪见皇帝,奏报履历,叫"引见",目的在于选拔效忠皇帝的臣仆。清朝嘉庆皇帝和咸丰皇帝(1850～1861年在位)曾在此举行过君臣抱见礼。嘉庆二年(1797年)都统额勒登保镇压了白莲教起义,咸丰五年参赞大臣僧格林沁镇压了捻军起义,都曾至御前举行过抱见礼。封建社会大臣见皇帝要行三拜九叩大礼,抱见礼是君臣手臂相扶,这是一种特殊的恩遇。

养心殿东、西暖阁是批阅奏章和召见大臣的地方。清朝奏事之制,各部院官员的奏摺,需经景运门内的外奏事处,转乾清门西庑的内奏事处,再由奏事太监转呈皇帝御览,皇帝批阅后,再由奏事官送出。

养心殿后殿即是皇帝的寝宫。寝宫东侧的体顺堂,为皇后侍寝时居所;西侧的燕喜堂,是妃嫔们被召的临时住房。

闻名中外的慈禧太后踏进西六宫,一步步掌握权力后,养心殿和西六宫都被她打上了深深的烙印。

西六宫位于养心殿北,包括永寿宫、翊坤宫、储秀宫、太极殿、长春宫和咸福宫,它们是明朝妃嫔的住所,清朝则后妃都可以住。

咸丰二年(1852年),清宫按惯例选八旗秀女,被选中的秀女有一位叶赫那拉氏,她小名兰儿,进宫后被封为兰贵人,住储秀宫后殿。咸丰四年晋为懿嫔,咸丰六年在此生下了唯一的皇子载淳,被晋封为懿妃,第二年又进封为懿贵妃。从此,她逐步插手政事,甚至代皇帝批阅奏折,飞扬跋扈,不可一世。

咸丰十一年七月,皇帝驾崩于承德避暑山庄,六岁的载淳即位,是为同治皇帝。母以子贵,懿贵妃被尊为圣母皇太后,人称慈禧太后。咸丰帝的皇后被尊为母后皇太后,即慈安太后。权力欲极强的慈禧太后,拉拢生性软弱、不谙政事的慈安太后,发动了"辛酉政变",夺得政权,实行垂帘听政。

养心殿东暖阁即是两太后垂帘听政的地方。慈禧太后实际上成了女皇帝。她借口皇帝年幼,需要照料,不住太后应该住的慈宁宫,而住在养心殿的燕喜堂。同治帝大婚后亲政,才移居长春宫。

同治十三年(1874年)小皇帝亲政不久就死了,慈禧太后又炮制了一个小皇帝光绪,继续垂帘听政,仍居燕喜堂。

光绪十年(1884年)十月十日慈禧太后五十大寿,提前五天在长春宫对面的戏台上天天演戏,近支王公、大臣、贵妇也被召进宫来看戏。并且在前一年就令重修储秀、体和、翊坤宫殿,耗银六十三万两。为了大办庆寿活动,于寿辰时,由长春宫移居储秀宫。如今储秀宫仍保持着慈禧太后五十大寿时的原貌。

慈禧太后住储秀宫时,在体和殿进膳。清朝皇帝平时进餐称进膳或传膳。每日正餐两顿,上午六、七点左右进早膳,下午一点半左右进"晚膳",晚上六点左右进晚点。各种"克食"(点心)可随时传叫。慈禧太后每餐有主食五十余种,菜一百二十多样,由四百五十人侍候。吃饭前还有专人尝膳,饭菜内都要放置长一寸的银牌,以防中毒。

本应是皇帝和后妃们活动的养心殿、西六宫,却处处晃动着慈禧太后的身影,这里是游客们探访禁宫生活的最佳去处。

The Hall of Mental Cultivation and the Six Western Palaces

Shaped like the letter "工" the Hall of Mental Cultivation (Yangxindian) stands in a large compound south of the Six Western Palaces. During the Qing Dynasty it was the second most important place in the Imperial Palace, only next to the Hall of Supreme Harmony. The front part of the hall was used as the office and the rear part as the bedroom of the emperor. The officials who were to be promoted, transfered or whose tenure of office was to expire were presented to the emperor by the Minister of Interior in this hall. On this occasion the officials had to be on their knees before the emperor while making a detailed report of antecedents. In 1797 Marshal Erledengbao suppressed the uprising of the Society of White Lotus and in 1856 Minister Sungelinqing put down the uprising of Nian Army. To reward the two generals for their meritorious deeds, Emperor Jia Qing and Emperor Xian Feng respectively accorded them heart-warming receptions. In the feudal dynasties, when the officials were received by the emperor, they had to bow three times and kowtow nine times. But as the emperor and the army commander met in the Hall of Mental Cultivation they held each other's arms, which was a very special honor.

The West Warm Chamber and East Warm Chamber of the Hall of Mental Cultivation were where the emperor read official reports and met high-ranking officials. During the Qing Dynasty memorials to the throne from various offices were first sent to two collecting points and then brought to the emperor by special eunuch messengers.

On the eastern side of the rear part of the hall is Tishuntang, where the empress would stay when she accompanied the emperor at night. On the western side of the rear part of th hall is Yanxitang, where imperial concubines would stay when they accompanied the emperor at night.

The Six Western Palaces are located north of the Hall of Mental Cultivation. They are the Palace of Eternal Longevity (Yongshougong), the Palace of Assisting the Empress (Yukungong), the Palace of Gatherng Elegance (Chuxiugong), the Hall of Evolution (Taijidian), the Palace of Eternal Spring (Changchungong), and the Palace of Cultivating Happiness (Xianfugong). During the Ming Dynasty they were the residence of imperial concubines. In the Qing Dynasty some empresses lived here too.

Empress Dowager Ci Xi was only a palace maid when she entered the palace in 1853. She became an imperial concubine and was promoted to be Lady Lan. After she gave birth to the only son of Emperor Xian Feng her rank was further raised twice. Ci Xi was interested in state affairs and the emperor allowed her to read official memorials and make decisions on behalf of him.

Emperor Xian Feng died on August 22, 1861. His six-year-old son succeeded to the crown with the reign title Tong Zhi. Ci Xi, the child emperor's mother, and weak-minded Ci An, Xian Feng's empress, deprived the power of the eight ministers who had been given regentship by Xian Feng, and proclaimed to the whole country that they would hold court behind the curtain. This is known as the 1861 Coup in history. The East Warm Chamber of the Hall of Mental Cultivation became the court of the two empress dowagers. Ci Xi, on the pretext that the young emperor needed his mother's care, lived in Yanxitang of the Hall of Mental Cultivation instead of the Palace of Motherly Tranquility, the usual residence of empress dowagers. She moved to the Palace of Eternal Spring only after Emperor Tong Zhi was married and formally took the reign of the country.

Tong Zhi died in 1874 at the age of 19. Ci Xi appointed a four-year-old child as the successor to the throne. She moved to stay in Yanxitang again and resumed her rule behind the curtain. To celebrate her 50th birthday, Empress Dowager Ci Xi gave the order to renovate and redecorate the Palace of Gathering Elegance, the Hall of Displaying Harmony and the Palace of Assisting the Empress one year earlier for the occasion. Altogether 630,000 taels of silver was spent on the project. In order to celebrate her birthday in a big way, Ci Xi moved from the Palace of Eternal Spring to the Palace of Gathering Elegance. Today the furniture and the decorations in the Palace of Gathering Elegance still look the same as on Ci Xi's 50th birthday.

When Ci Xi lived in the Palace of Gathering Elegance she had her meals in the Hall of Displaying Harmony. In those days, breakfast was served at 6:30 a. m., lunch at 12, dinner at 6 p. m. More than 50 kinds of staple food and 120 courses were prepared for each meal. Ci Xi was waited on by 450 attendants when she ate. Before she started eating, an attendant would come forward and taste each dish to see if it was poisonous. A small piece of silver tablet, about one inch long, was put inside each bowl as an indicator of poisoned food.

Visitors can find traces of Ci Xi's life everywhere in the Hall of Mental Cultivation and the Six Western Palaces.

养心门 即养心殿的大门。为庑殿式门楼，楼顶及左右"八"字影壁均镶嵌着琉璃构件，门外置一对鎏金铜狮，整个门面端庄典雅，气派华贵。

Gate of Mental Cultivation (Yangxinmen) The main entrance to the Hall of Mental Cultivation has a gable roof. The screen walls flanking it are decorated with patterns of glazed tiles. Two gilded bronze lions sit at either side of the gate.

养心殿　位于西六宫南,建于明代,清雍正年间改建。殿内陈设讲究,是雍正皇帝以后历代皇帝处理政务和居住的地方。每天清晨,皇帝在此接见军机大臣,听取政务。慈禧太后揽权期间所谓"垂帘听政"就在这里。

Hall of Mental Cultivation (Yangxindian) The hall was first built in the Ming Dynasty and rebuilt under the reign of Yong Zheng of the Qing Dynasty. The Qing emperors after Yong Zheng all handled state affairs here. Every morning they would receive important ministers in this hall. Empress Dowager Ci Xi ruled China behind the certain in this hall.

养心殿大堂 堂内设宝座，上悬"中正仁和"匾，为雍正皇帝御题。这里是皇帝召见大臣、引见官员的地方。

Inside the Hall of Mental Cultivation In the main room of the front part hangs a horizontal board bearing the Chinese characters for "Just and Benevolent" in Emperor Yong

Zheng's handwriting. This is
where the emperor gave audience to his ministers and officials to be promoted or
transfered.

养心殿东暖阁　这里是"辛酉政变"后慈安、慈禧两太后"垂帘听政"的地方。黄色纱帘前后设两个宝座，小皇帝坐帘前，仅作摆设，一切军政大事均由帘内太后决定。六岁的同治皇帝和四岁的光绪皇帝先后在此充当傀儡。

East Warm Chamber After the 1861 Coup Empress Dowagers Ci Xi and Ci An took over the power and began to "hold court behind the certain". First the 6-year-old child emperor Tong Zhi, and then, after Tong Zhi died, the 4-year-old child emperor Guang Xi were seated on the throne in front, while the two empress dowagers were seated on the large throne behind. There was a yellow gauze curtain between the two thrones.

皇帝寝宫 图为寝宫外间,隔扇内为皇帝卧室。清代自雍正皇帝以后,历代皇帝均居此。室内"天行健"、"自强不息"匾额均为光绪皇帝手笔。

Bedroom of the Emperor The bedroom behind the screen was for all the Qing emperors after Yong Zheng. The two inscriptions on the horizontal boards in Emperor Guang Xu's handwriting read: "The Heavenly Law Is Powerful" and "Be Diligent".

龙床 皇帝自诩为"真龙天子",其卧床称为"龙床"。床楣所悬"又日新"匾为慈禧太后所书,其意为保持德行日贤于一日。

Dragon Bed The emperor claimed he was the dragon. So his bed was called dragon bed.

The inscription above the bed is in the handwriting of Empress Dowager Ci Xi, meaning to retain virtue.

储秀宫 西六宫之一,位于西六宫西北角。慈禧太后发迹前曾以贵人身份入住后殿,并在此生下同治皇帝。民国初年,溥仪的皇后婉容曾入居此宫。

Palace of Gathering Elegance (Chuxiugong) It stands in the northwestern corner of the Six Western Palaces. Empress Dowager Ci Xi moved to live here after she was promoted to Ladyship and gave birth to the future Emperor Tong Zhi. In the early Republic the dethroned emperor Pu Yi and his wife Wan Rong once lived in this palace.

储秀宫内景 储秀宫内装饰精巧华丽，为六宫之冠。正中设宝座，是慈禧太后接受朝贺的地方。

Inside the Palace of Gathering Elegance This place is the best embellished in the Inner Court. Empress Dowager Ci Xi sat on the throne to receive greetings from high-ranking officials.

慈禧太后"龙床" 床设檀木葫芦炕罩，其上透雕子孙万代图案。床上铺锦绣缎被，张挂三层苏绣幔帐，皆为五彩缎绸所做。如此奢华的床上铺设，在宫中仅此一处。

"Dragon Bed of Ci Xi" On the bed is a screen of sandalwood carved with many young boys. The quilts, mattresses and three layers of drapery are of colorful silk and satin. This bed is the most extravagantly decorated in the Imperial Palace.

象牙船 存放于储秀宫内，共两只，一为龙形，一为凤状。船长91.5厘米，宽35厘米，高58厘米，船上雕刻着福、禄、寿三星及群仙众神共四十二个人物，其形象逼真，活灵活现，堪称艺术精品。这两件珍宝是大臣们在千秋节恭奉给慈禧太后的寿礼。

Ivory Boats The Palace of Gathering Elegance has two ivory boats, one in the shape of a dragon and the other in the shape of a phoenix. Both are 91.5 centimeters long, 35 centimeters wide and 58 centimeters high. Forty-two immortals are carved on the boats. They were birthday presents of court ministers to Empress Dowager Ci Xi.

珍宝馆和钟表馆

故宫东北部有一组宏伟的宫殿建筑群叫宁寿全宫,举世瞩目的珍宝馆就设在其主殿——皇极殿内。

宁寿全宫俗称外东路,明朝和清初是太后、太妃们居住的宫殿,清乾隆皇帝为了归政以后颐养而大规模扩修。乾隆皇帝继位之初即声言,不愿自己在位的年限超越其祖康熙皇帝(康熙帝在位六十一年),如能坐满六十年皇位,则禅位皇太子。为此,乾隆三十七年(1772 后)动工修建自己禅位后的太上皇宫殿,这就是宁寿全宫。

宁寿全宫分前后两部分。前半部以皇极殿、宁寿宫为主,是太上皇接受群臣朝贺处;后半部分三路,正中一路以养性殿、乐寿堂为主,东有畅音阁和阅是楼一组燕乐建筑,西为乾隆花园。

嘉庆元年(1796 年)正月初一,乾隆皇帝达到了初愿,传位第十五子颙琰。初四,太上皇在皇极殿赐千叟宴。

千叟宴是一种规模浩大的宴会。清朝二百多年间,仅康乾盛世举行过四次,嘉庆元年是规模最大的一次。六十岁以上的三品以上官员、六十五岁以上的三品以下官员以及七十岁以上的其他老者皆可入宴。

此次千叟宴,耆老入宴者达三千五百余人,列名邀赏者达五千余人。尚有蒙古、回部、番部、朝鲜等国贺正使节。特准所有与宴官员军民年九十以上者由子孙搀扶入宴;文武大臣年逾七旬者,如步履维艰,亦准子孙一人搀扶入宴,故与宴者总数超过八千之众。

　是日晨,礼部预先在皇极殿宝座前设太上皇和嗣皇帝御宴金龙宴桌,加黄幕帷罩。以御宴席为中心,左右两路相对设宴桌,每路六排,每排二十二至一百席不等,共设八百席。一、二品以上大臣在殿内,外国使臣在殿廊下,三品大臣在丹陛甬道两旁,四品以下官在丹墀左右,九品以下人等在宁寿门外甬路两旁就宴。各宴桌均加青幕帷罩,按等级和规定摆上各种珍馐。

　酒宴开始,太上皇捧起酒杯一饮而尽。皇帝到宝座前跪受爵,递与进爵大臣后入座。太上皇当即召与宴王公、一品大臣及众叟中年届九十以上者至御宴前跪,亲赐卮酒、普加赏赉,并各加赏缎疋、银锞等;还对高寿一百零六岁的安徽老民熊国沛、百岁山东老民梁廷玉特别加恩,赏给六品顶戴花翎,另赏九十以上老者七人七品顶戴花翎。此时诸皇子皇孙等为殿内宗室王公敬酒,侍卫等为殿檐下、丹墀上下及甬道左右各席群臣众叟敬酒。八千老叟于座旁行一叩礼后开始进餐。宴毕,与宴人众再行一跪三叩礼,谢恩。宴后,又按品级或年龄,分赐诗刻、如意、寿杖、朝珠等物。真是旷古少有的大盛事!

　曾经盛况空前的皇极殿,如今摆上了各种明清宫廷珍品,每日游人如织,再现了空前盛况。

　位于珍宝馆西南的钟表馆是吸引游人的又一个好去处,内藏十八、十九世纪清宫收藏的各种钟表。其造型丰富多彩:乱真的园林楼阁,惟妙惟肖的人物,栩栩如生的鸟兽,生机勃勃的花木装饰,令人目不暇接,其中大部分钟表制造精细,机关设置灵巧,不仅能准确计时,还能演奏悠扬宛转的乐曲,也能模仿人物和动物各种杂耍表演,令人叹为观止。

The Hall of Jewelry and the Hall of Clocks

The exhibition room of jewelry is located in the Hall of Imperial Supremacy, the main building of the Outer Eastern Palaces. In the Ming Dynasty and early Qing Dynasty the Outer Eastern Palaces were the residence of the empress dowager and the concubines of the deceased monarch. Emperor Qian Long of the Qing Dynasty ascended the throne at the age of 25. He promised he would renounce the throne in favor of his son after he had ruled for 60 years, because he didn't want to have his reign last longer than that of his grandfather Kang Xi (Kang Xi had ruled for 61 years). Qian Long extended the buildings in the Outer Eastern Palaces, so that he might live there after he resigned the sovereign authority. The general plan of this group of buildings is made exactly after that on the central axis of the Imperial Palace: three big halls in the Outer Court and three palaces in the Inner Court. Retired Emperor Qian Long received festive greetings from officials in the Outer Court. The Inner Court was the residence of the retired emperor and his empress. West of the palaces is Qian Long's Garden.

On the first day of the first lunar month of the 60th year of Qian Long's reign, a grand ceremony was performed to retire the old emperor and crown the new emperor. Four days later, Qian Long, the supersovereign, gave a banquet to entertain 3,500 aged men at the Hall of Imperial Supremacy, the grandest one of the four Thousand-Old-Men Banquets Qian Long gave during his reign. To make the emperor's appearance more impressive and add to the joyful atmosphere, orchestras were disposed along the veranda of the hall and off the Gate of

Tranquil Longevity. The age limit for the guests was set as follows: 60 or older for officials above the third rank; 65 or older for officials under the third rank; 70 or older for the rest of the guests. Those over 90 could have a son or a grandson to help them; those high-ranking officials who had difficulty in walking and more than 70 years old could also have a son or grandson to help them. Together with foreign envoys there were more than 8,000 people at the banquet.

Altogether 800 tables were laid for the banquet. Inside the main hall, gold-dragon tables were set before the throne for Qian Long and his son Jia Qing. Besides there were 38 tables for princes, dukes, marquises and officials of the first rank; 366 tables were spread in the veranda for officials of the second rank and foreign envoys; 60 tables were put on both sides of the central passageway for officials of the third rank; 240 tables were places on the right and left side of the marble terrace for officials of the 4th or 5th rank and Mongol guests, 200 tables were set out outside the Gate of Tranquil Longevity for officials of the 6th to 9th rank; and another 200 tables were laid outside the Gate of Imperial Supremacy for retired guards, soldiers, artisans and ordinary citizens. The oldest guest who attended the banquet was Xiong Guopei, aged 106, from Anhui Province. The supersovereign conferred on him and 100-year-old Liang Tingyu from Shandong Province the honorary official title of 6th rank and those over 90 years old the official title of 7th rank. He also gave presents to all the guests. Today the Hall of Imperial Supremacy displays many treasures from the Ming and Qing dynasties.

The Hall of Clocks is located to the southwest of the Hall of Jewelry. This exhibition room keeps clocks collected by the Qing imperial court in the 18th and 19th centuries. Some are in the shape of a tower, a human figure, a bird or an animal; some are embellished with flowers and plants; some can play music or mimic human or animal movements. Exquisitely made, these clocks still run accurately.

钟表馆 设在明清皇家供奉祖宗的奉先殿,内藏近代各式钟表 182 件。

Hall of Clocks This exhibition room is located inside the Hall of Worshipping Ancestors. It keeps 182 clocks collected by the Qing imperial court.

铜壶滴漏 为中国古代计时器,俗称漏壶,由日天壶、夜天壶、平水壶、分水壶和受水壶五部分构成。此壶至今完好无损,为故宫珍品。

Water Clock The clepsydra is a time-piece used in ancient China. It is composed of five bronze vessels, each has a small hole at the bottom. When the uppermost vessel is filled with water, it begins to drip evenly through the holes.

九龙壁 是清代现存三座九龙壁之一,位于皇极门前。壁高3.5米,宽29.4米,由270块彩色琉璃件构成,壁面九龙姿态各异,飞腾嬉戏于海涛云气之中,颇有呼之欲出的感觉。

Nine-Dragon Screen Three Nine-Dragon Screens of the Qing Dynasty have been left in China. This one in the Outer Eastern Palaces is 3.5 meters high, 29.4 meters long and built with 270 glazed multi-colored tiles. Nine dragons romp in the sea against a background of waves, cliffs and clouds.

珍宝馆　设在皇极殿，殿内陈列着明清两代皇室珍宝，包括皇帝、后妃们使用的服饰、金银器物，各种珠宝盆景和金、玉质料的装饰品。藏品数量之多，价值之高，世所罕见。

Hall of Jewelry On display in this exhibition room are dressing ornaments and gold and silver objects used by the emperors, empresses and imperial concubines during the Ming and Qing dynasties. There are also miniature landscapes made of jewelry and a great number of treasures.

象牙席　为稀世珍宝，席长 216 厘米，宽 139 厘米，制做此席须精选象牙，将象牙作特殊处理，然后劈成厚 0.1 厘米，宽 0.3 厘米的象牙条，编织成席。清雍正年间曾制做五件，现存三件。

Ivory Mat It is 216 centimeters by 139 centimeters and woven of ivory filaments less than 0.3 centimeter wide and 0.1 centimeter thick. Five ivory mats were made during the reign of Yong Zheng. Three have remained.

"大禹治水"玉雕　是中国现存最大的玉雕,表现上古大禹治水的故事。成品高 2.24 米,重 5 吨。玉料采自新疆,运至扬州雕琢,琢成后运回北京,前后耗时十余年。

'Yu, the Great Harnessing Floods' The largest piece of jade carving in China today, it is 2. 24 meters high and weighs five tons. This huge block of jade was quarried in Xinjiang and transported to Yangzhou. After the carving was finished there it was shipped to Beijing. The whole process took ten years.

朝服 是清代皇帝的重要礼服之一，有明黄、蓝、红和月白四种颜色，元旦、万寿节、祭祀太庙等重大庆典时穿明黄色朝服。朝服上除有云龙纹饰外，还有日、月、星辰、山、龙、华虫、黼、黻、宗彝、藻、火、粉米等十二章图案，寓意皇帝代天行政，普照四方。

Ceremonial Dress The emperor of the Qing Dynasty had four sets of dresses for grand ceremonies; one yellow, one blue, one red and one white. The emperor put on the yellow dress on New Year's Day, Longevity Festival and when he offered sacrifice at the Temple of Ancestors. The dresses bear designs of dragons, clouds, sun, moon, stars, sea weeds, flames and others to imply that the emperor ruled on behalf of Heaven.

凤冠 为皇后参加重大庆典时所戴礼服冠。图中凤冠由珍珠宝石和黄金制成，正中三只金凤不仅是美丽的装饰品，也是皇后与妃嫔区别等级的重要标志。

Phoenix Crown The empress put on this crown on important occasions. It is made of pearls, precious stones and gold filaments. The three phoenixes are the symbol of the empress. Other imperial consorts were not allowed to wear this crown.

乾隆花园一角 乾隆花园位于宁寿全宫西北部,共四进院落。园内庭院衔联,叠石为山,松竹布景,亭轩点染。漫步园中,步移景换,涉门成趣,其乐无穷。

Qian Long's Garden The garden is located in the northwestern part of the Outer Eastern Palaces and consists of four small courtyards. Artificial hills built with rocks are seen everywhere, and pines, cypresses and bamboo groves add great beauty to the garden.

107

禊赏亭流杯渠　渠深 10 厘米，作如意形环绕。每逢三月上巳节，人们将酒杯漂浮水面，宛转曲流，享受泛觞之乐。

Cup-Floating Canal in Xishang Pavilion Wine cups would be floated along the winding 10-centimeter-deep canal cut into the rock floor during a festival held in the spring, meaning to cleanse away evil influences.

珍妃井 位于宁寿全宫北端，因珍妃而得名。珍妃是光绪皇帝的宠妃，因支持皇帝新政被打入冷宫。1900年八国联军攻入北京，慈禧太后外逃前令太监推入此井溺死，年仅二十五岁。

Zhenfei's Well Zhenfei was Emperor Guang Xu's favorite concubine, but she was on bad terms with Empress Dowager Ci Xi for she supported the 1898 Reform Movement. In 1900 the Allied Forces of Eight Foreign Powers invaded Beijing. Before her fleeing Ci Xi ordered an eunuch to push Zhenfei into the well to be drowned. Then she was only 25 years old.

御花园

　　御花园，位于坤宁门后，明代称宫后苑，始建于永乐十五年(1417年)。花园座落于纵贯紫禁城南北中轴线的北端，占地约1.3公顷，是北京最古老、最有特色、最具代表性的宫廷花园。清朝，帝后于七月七日在御花园祭祀牛郎、织女星；八月中秋夜在此祭月；九九重阳登园中堆秀山居高揽景。

　　自坤宁门步入御花园，园中松柏苍翠，花木扶疏，山石、陈设争奇竞秀，亭台殿阁错落有致，呈现出一派清幽绚丽的景色，与宫廷严整肃穆的气氛形成鲜明的对比。

　　御花园以位于中轴线上的钦安殿为中心，东有万春、浮碧、凝香，西有千秋、澄瑞、玉翠等亭，它们从形式到布局都讲究工整对称，甚至命名也东西对仗，如万春对千秋，浮碧对澄瑞，凝香对玉翠。这种布局，在园林建筑中本应极力避免，但在御花园中却力求工整对应。因为只有左右对称的布局，才能突出贯穿南北的轴线，与宫廷区的其他建筑群融为一体。聪明的古代工匠采取了保持建筑的基本对称，而改变主景和环境布置的方法，保持了宫廷建筑的整体格调。

　　园东北区主景是嶙峋怪石叠成的堆秀山，山顶置御景亭，登山入亭，近可观园中秀色，远可看宫廷美景。摛藻堂傍山面水，呈现一种清幽安适的气氛；浮碧亭与堆秀山相望，引出一种山青水秀的意境；稍远处的万春亭在山景的衬托下也另有一番韵味。而西北区的主景是巍峨秀丽的延晖阁，以阁为景观中心,阁前古柏成行,构成一幅幅楼亭起伏、檐宇错落的画面,产生一种幽深恬静的气氛。这一山一阁的安排,对御花园环境的烘托起了出神入化的作用。

山石树木、花池盆景也是御花园造景的重要手法之一,尤其是园中那条彩色石子路,给人们带来另一番情趣。这条回旋于翠竹、松柏、花丛之中长一公里的小路,是由近千幅生动的画面和连续图案组成的。图案内容丰富多采,诸如四季百花"喜鹊报春"、"凤垂牡丹"等,吉祥图案"连中三元"、"五子登科"、"五福捧寿"等;历史故事"回荆卅"、"过五关斩六将"等;还有民间传说"张生戏莺莺"、"二老观棋"等等,每一画面都刻画得形象逼真、栩栩如生。其中尤以反映民间生活的"怕媳图"最为有趣。画面表现泼妇罚夫,有的男子跪在板凳上,头顶着灯;有的男子跪在搓板上,头顶着板凳,妻子连打带骂;还有一男子骑着毛驴,其妻步行随后,使受罚的男子羡慕不已,问:你妻对你怎如此之好?让你骑驴,她走路。答曰:昨夜腿被吾妻打断,今骑驴去医治。种种情态,令观者忍俊不禁。

这条辗转相连的花石子路与园中楼亭池榭、参天古柏、争艳百花融为一体,形成皇家园林特有的风貌。

Imperial Garden

The Imperial Garden, built in 1417, is the oldest garden in Beijing. It occupies an area of 1.3 hectares at the northern end of the central axis of the former Imperial Palace. During the Qing Dynasty the emperor, empress and imperial concubines came to the garden to worship the Cowherd Star and the Girl Weaver Star on the 7th day of the 7th lunar month. On the Mid-Autumn Festival they came here to offer a sacrifice to the moon, and on the Double-Ninth Festival (the 9th day of the 9th lunar month) they came here to ascend the Hill of Collecting Excellence in the garden and enjoy scenic beauty within and outside the Imperial Palace.

The main scenic spot in the northeastern part is the Hill of Collecting Excellence. The Pavilion of Imperial Landscape stands on the hill. In front of Li Zao Hall by the hill is a small pond of clear water. The main scenic spot in the northwestern part is the Pavilion of Lasting Splendor. In front of the pavilion there are some ancient cypress trees over 400 years old.

A pathway in the Imperial Garden arouses great interest among visitors. The one-kilometer-long path is paved with pebbles of various colors, composing nearly 1,000 pictures and designs and snakes its way between bamboo groves, pines, cypresses and plants. The designs cover a wide range of subjects, such as episodes from classic novels, folk tales and auspicious symbols. Some pictures reflecting the life of ordinary people are very amusing. One of them is "Henpecked Husbands", which depicts two husbands, one with an oil lamp on his head, kneeling on a wooden bench, the other with a bench on his head, kneeling on a wash board, both being beaten by their wives. Another man is riding by on a donkey, followed by his wife on foot. Feeling envious, one of the kneeling men asks, "Why is your wife so nice to you? You are riding the donkey while she is walking behind." The man on the donkey answers, "You don't know the truth. She broke my leg when beating me last night. Now I have to ride the donkey to see the doctor."

Centering around the Hall of Imperial Peace (Qin'andian), the garden has over 10 pavilions, terraces and towers laid out in symmetry and beautifully embellished with fantastic rockeries, ancient cypress trees, bamboo groves and exotic flowering plants.

连理柏 实为异干异根、距今已有四百余年的两株古柏,柏枝纽结纠缠,树干相依相偎,颇似恋人幽会,其情缠绵,其状感人。

Twin Cypress Trees The two trees with their branches entwined look like two lovers embracing. They are more than 400 years old.

钦安殿 是御花园的主体建筑,也是故宫中轴线上唯一的宗教建筑。殿内供奉水神玄武,意在宫中避火消灾。

**The Hall of Imperial Peace
(Qin'andian)** Inside the hall
stands the statue of the King
of Xuan Wu flanked by bronze
statues, who was believed to
be the Water God and could,
therefore, prevent the palace
buildings from catching fire.

御景亭　位于钦安殿东北,建于由太湖石叠起的堆秀山顶,山的匾额"堆秀"、"云根"为乾隆皇帝御笔。每年九月九日重阳节,皇帝、后妃们登山入亭,了望紫禁城内外景色。

Imperial Sight Pavilion（Yu-jingting） The pavilion stands on an artificial hill of rocks from Taihu Lake. The inscriptions on two boards—"Collecting Excellence" and "Cloud Roots"—are in the handwriting of Emperor Qian Long. On the 9th day of the 9th lunar month the emperor and his consorts would ascend this height and enjoy the scenic beauty both within and outside the Imperial Palace.

金鱼戏睡莲 浮碧亭是堆秀山东侧一敞亭,亭下有一方形鱼池,池中睡莲花开,金鱼嬉戏其间,一静一动,绿肥红瘦,相映成趣。

Goldfish and Water Lilies It is a wonderful sight in summer when water lilies under the Pavilion of Floating Green are in blossom and goldfish swim among them.

119

神武门 为故宫北门，高 31 米。皇后、妃嫔们前往蚕坛举行亲蚕仪式出入此门。崇祯皇帝出此门逃往万岁山（即现在景山），吊死在槐树下。

Gate of Divine Prowess (Shenwumen) The north gate to the Imperial Palace is 31 meters high. The empress and imperial concubines left the palace through this gate to attend the ceremony of starting silkworm breeding season. Chong Zhen, the last emperor of the Ming Dynasty, went through this gate to hang himself on a tree at the Coal Hill.

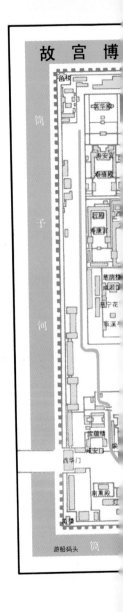

故 宫 博

角楼

英华殿

寿安宫

寿禧殿

巨殿

西

寿康宫

慈荫楼

咸若馆

慈宁花

临溪亭

宝蕴楼

咸安门

焕

西华门

南薰殿

灯

角楼

游船码头 筒

筒 子 河

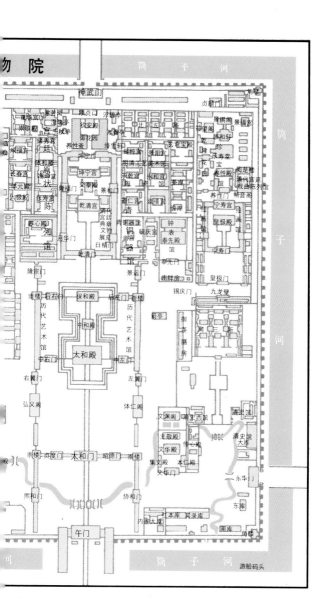

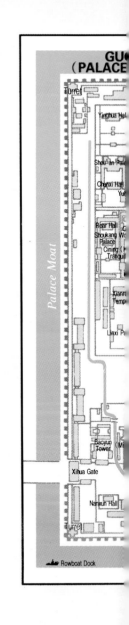

Turret

Yinghua Hall

Shou'an Palace

Chunxi Hall

Yu

Rear Hall
Shoukang
Palace
Cining (
Tranquil

Xianr
Temp

Linxi Pa

Baoyun
Tower (M

Xihua Gate

Nanxun Hall

Turret

Palace Moat

Rowboat Dock

Palace Moat

Turret

Shenwu (Spiritual Valour) Gate

Shufang Lodge

Chonqjing Hall

Jing House

Qin'an (Imperial Peace) Hall

North Five Abodes

Xuan Qiong Hall

Fuwang Belvedere

Jingfu Palace

Yihe House

Yanfu Palace

Imperial Garden

Hall of Arts and Crafts of the Ming and Qing Dynasties

Jeshou Pleasure and Longevity) Hall

ning Study

Kunning (Earthly Tranquillity) Palace

Yonghe Palace

Hall of Jewelry

chun Palace

Yangxing Hall

irxian Hall

Jiaotai (Union) Hall

Taiji Hall

Qianqing (Heavenly Purity) Palace

Yanxi Palace

Yangxing Gate

Yangxin (Mental Cultivation) Hall

Ningshou Palace

ddha

Huangji (Imperial Supremacy) Hall

Yuehua Gate

Rijing Gate

Fengxian (Serving of Ancestors) Hall

Hall of Paintings

Qianqing (Heavenly Purity) Gate

Ningshou Gate

Longzong Gate

Jingyun Gate

Hall of Bronzes

Baohe (Preserving Harmony) Hall

Nine – Dragon Screen

Zhonghe (Middle Harmony) Hall

Archery Pavilion

South – Three Abodes

Taihe (Supreme Harmony) Hall

Imperial Kitchen

Hongyi Pavilion

Tiren Pavilion

Wenyuan Pavilion (Imperial Library)

Qing Dynasty Archives

s) Lofty Tower

Taihe (Supreme Harmony) Gate

Lofty Tower

Wenhua (Literary Glory) Hall

Xihe Gate

Golden River Bridges

Xiehe Gate

Wenhua Gate

Donghua Gate

Cabinet Hall

Wumen Gate (Meridian Gate)

Turret

Moat

Palace Moat

Rowboat Dock

Palace Moat

编辑	施永南	
翻译	刘宗仁	
摄影	罗文发	望天星
	张肇基	高明义
	姜景余	胡维标
	王春树	牛嵩林
	任诗吟	刘思功
设计	望天星	

Edited by Shi Yongnan
Translated by Liu Zongren
Photos by Luo Wenfa, Wang Tianxing, Zhang Zhaoji, Gao Mingyi, Jiang Jingyu, Hu Weibiao, Wang Chunshu, Niu Songlin, Ren Shiyin and Liu Sigong
Designed by Wang Tianxing

（京）新登字 131 号

图书在版编目（CIP）数据

故宫导游手册:日、法文/熊凤台日译,曾培耿法译 . 北京:中国世界语出版社,1996.2

ISBN 7 - 5052 - 0279 - 0

I. 故…　II.①熊…　②曾…　III.①故宫 - 导游 - 手册 - 日文②故宫 - 导游 - 手册 - 法文　IV.K928.74 - 62

中国版本图书馆 CIP 数据核字(95)第 24402 号

故宫导游手册

*

中国世界语出版社出版

北京博诚印刷厂印制

（北京 1201 工厂）

中国国际图书贸易总公司(国际书店)发行

1996 年(36 开)第一版第一次印刷

ISBN 7 - 5052 - 0278 - 2/K.42(外)

17 - CE - 3083P

02000